Handwriting Practice for Kids

Muneet

Clever Kiddo

A is for

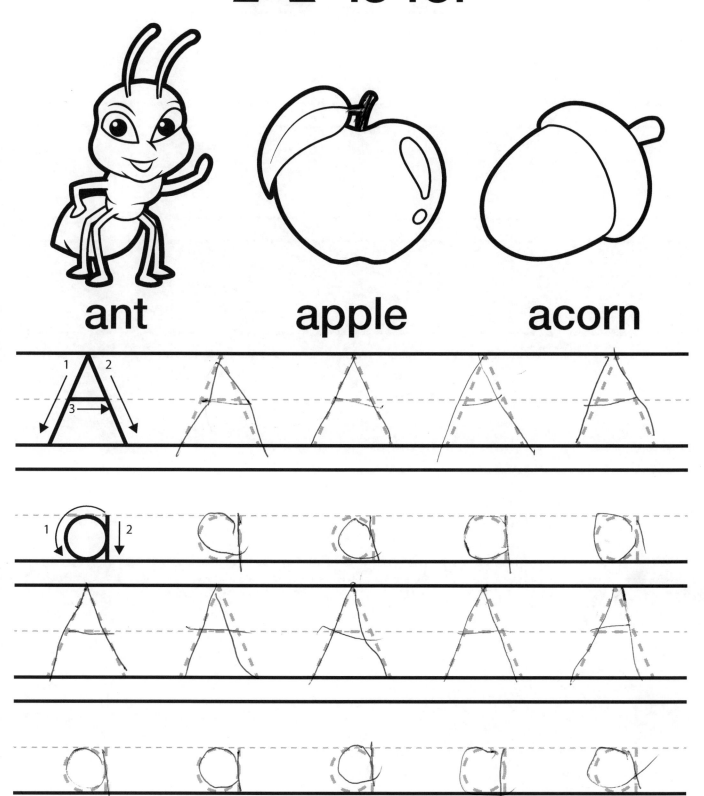

ant apple acorn

A A A A A

a a a a a

A A A A A

a a a a a

A A A A A

a a a a a

A A A A A

a a a a a

B is for

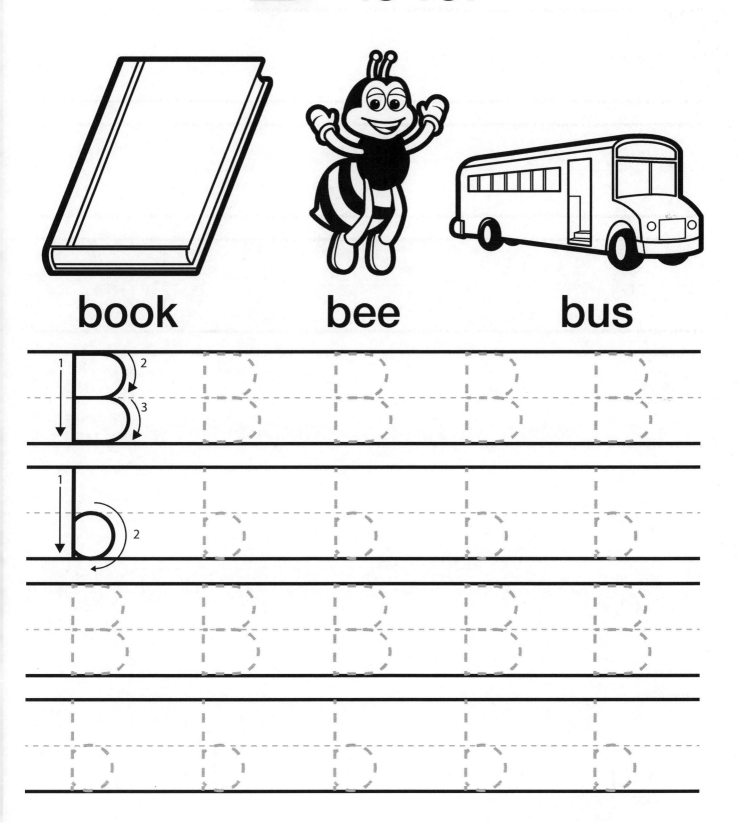

book   bee   bus

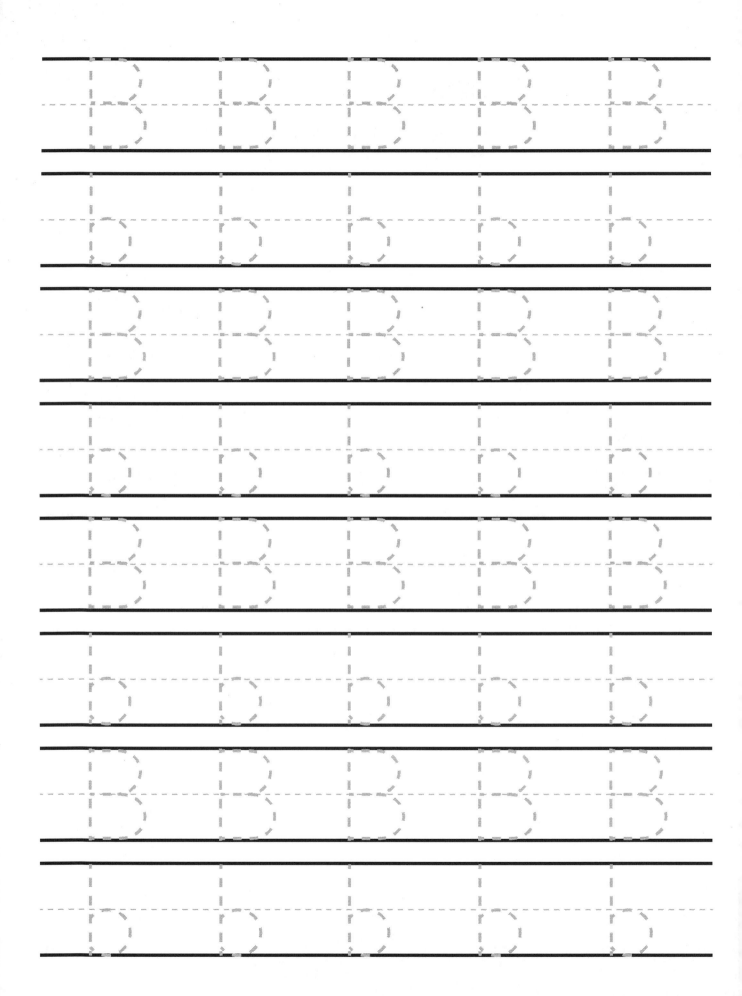

C is for

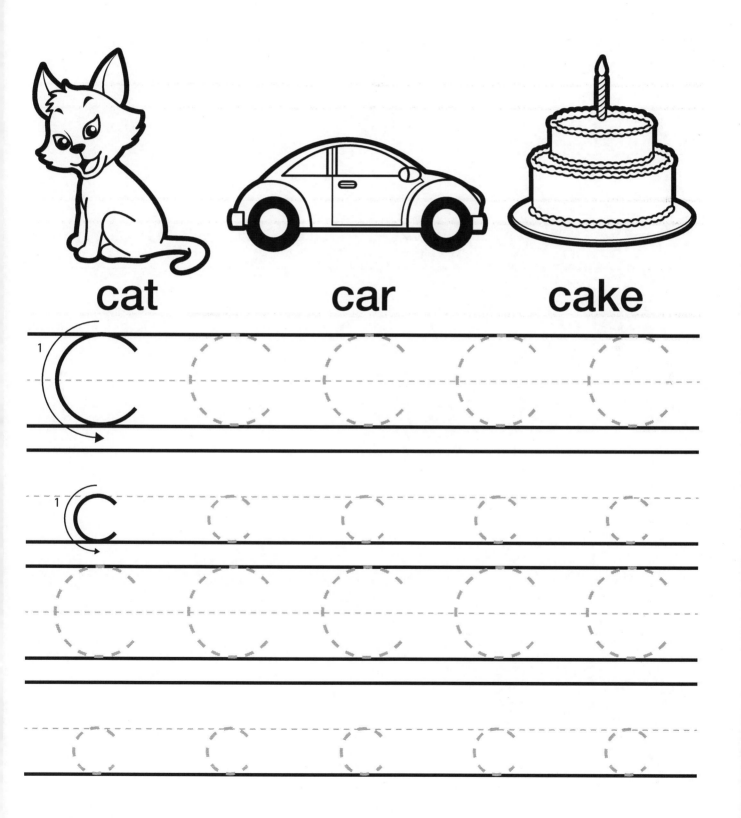

cat   car   cake

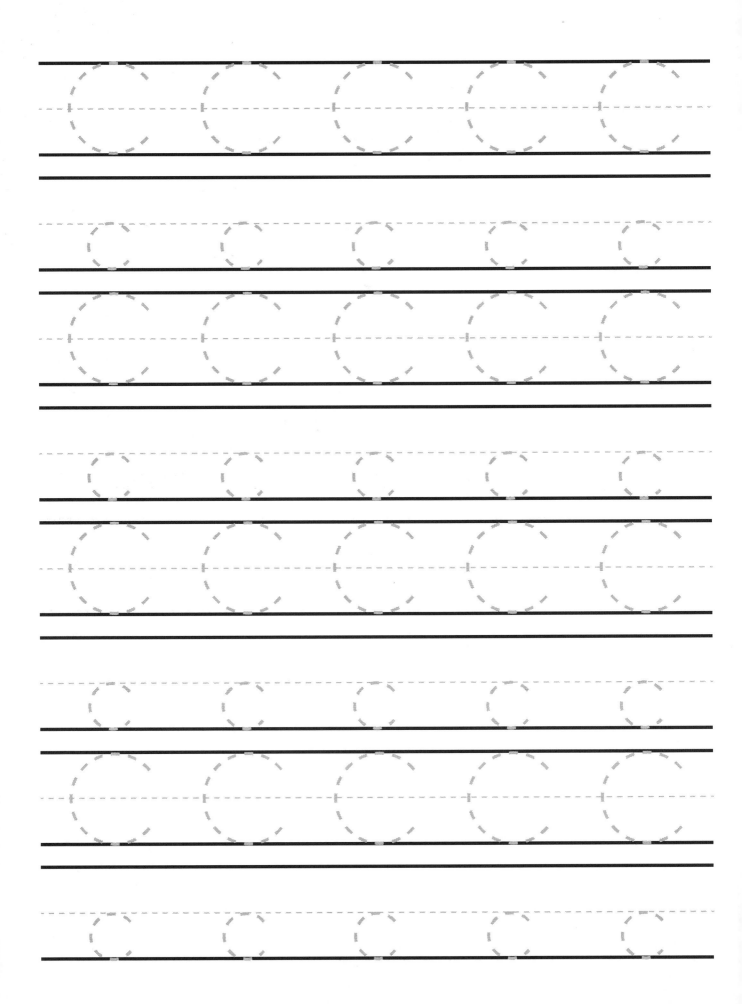

D is for

dog

doll

dinosaur

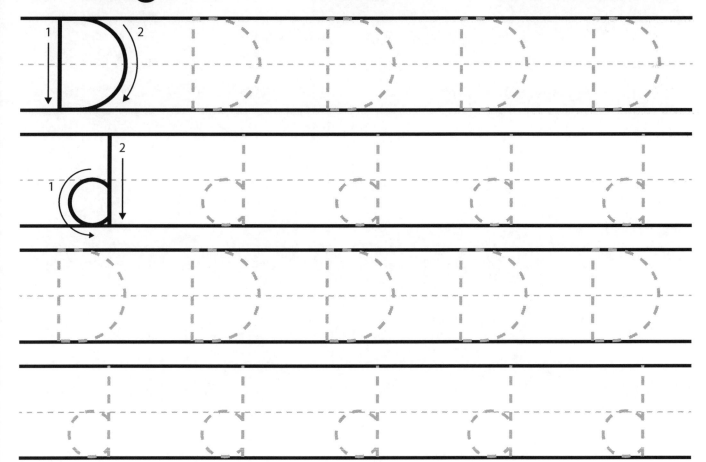

E is for

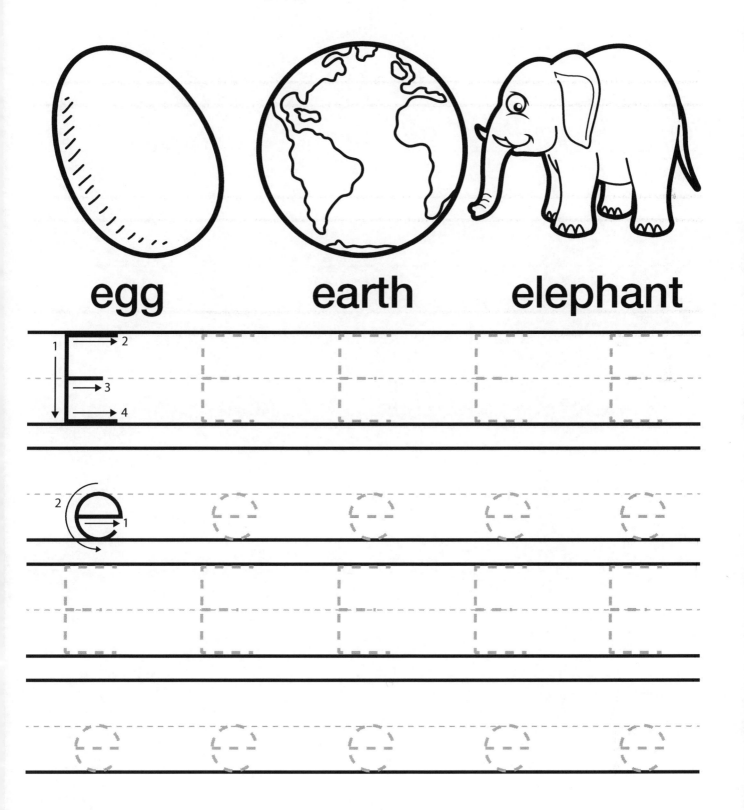

egg   earth   elephant

F is for

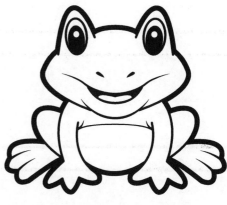

fish   flower   frog

G is for

goat

girl

giraffe

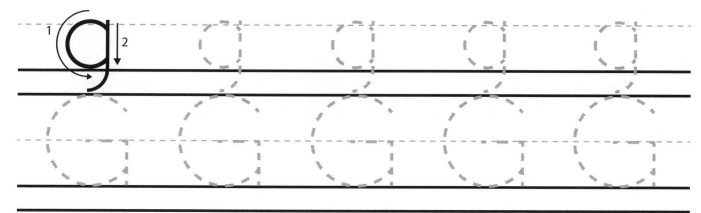

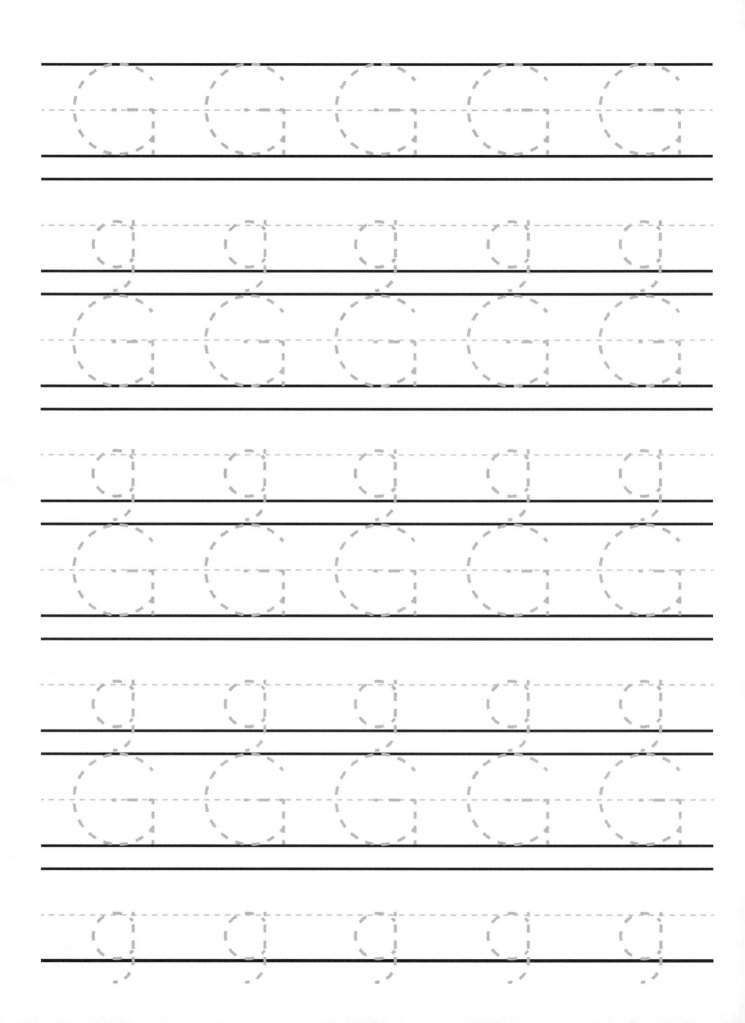

H is for

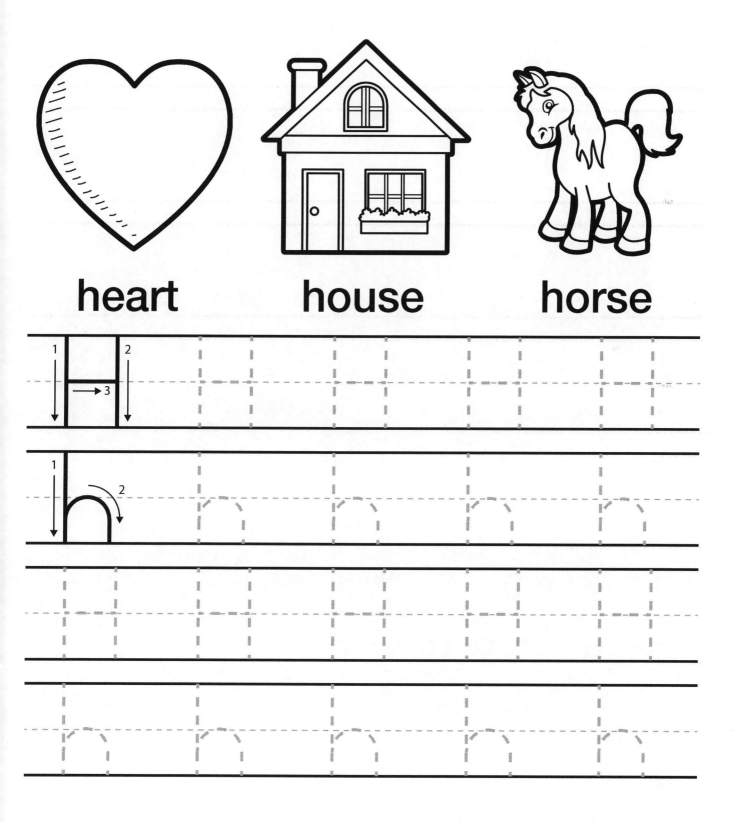

heart   house   horse

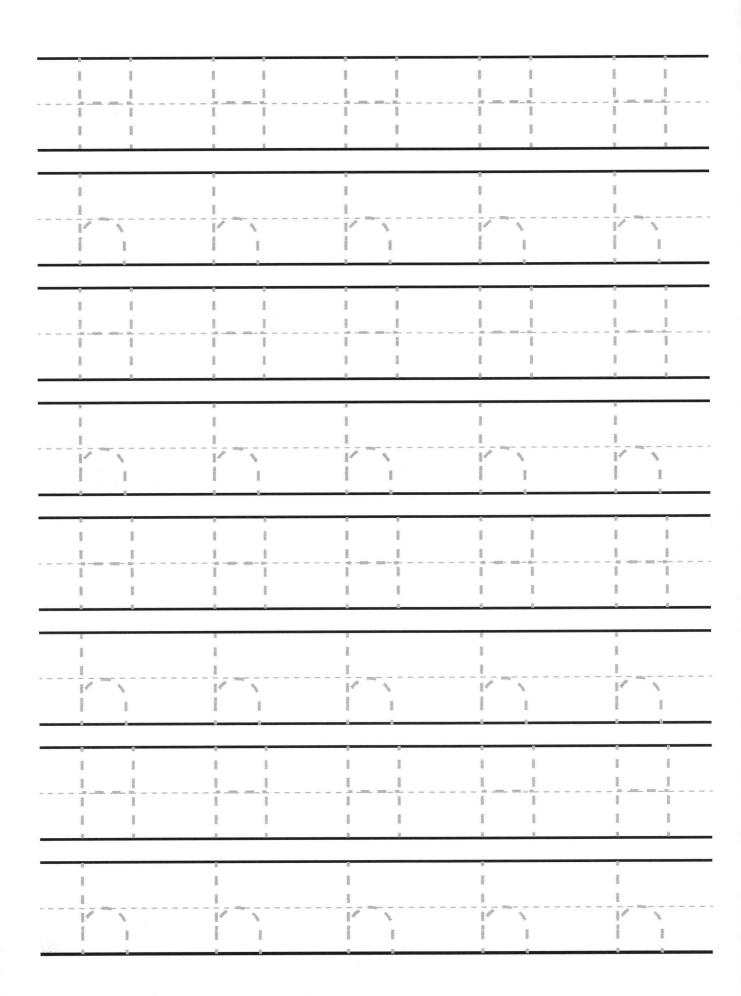

 is for

ice cream   iguana   island

J is for

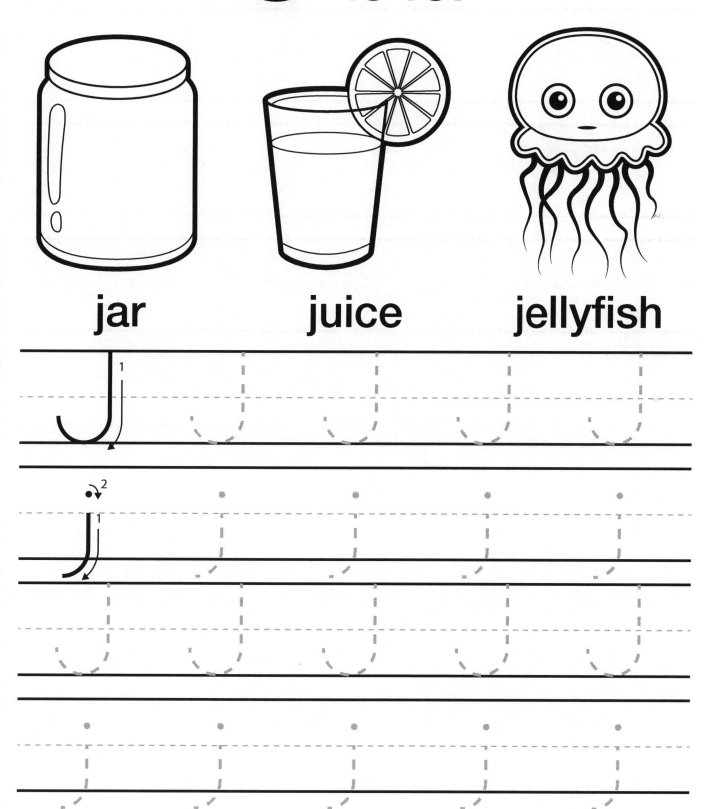

jar   juice   jellyfish

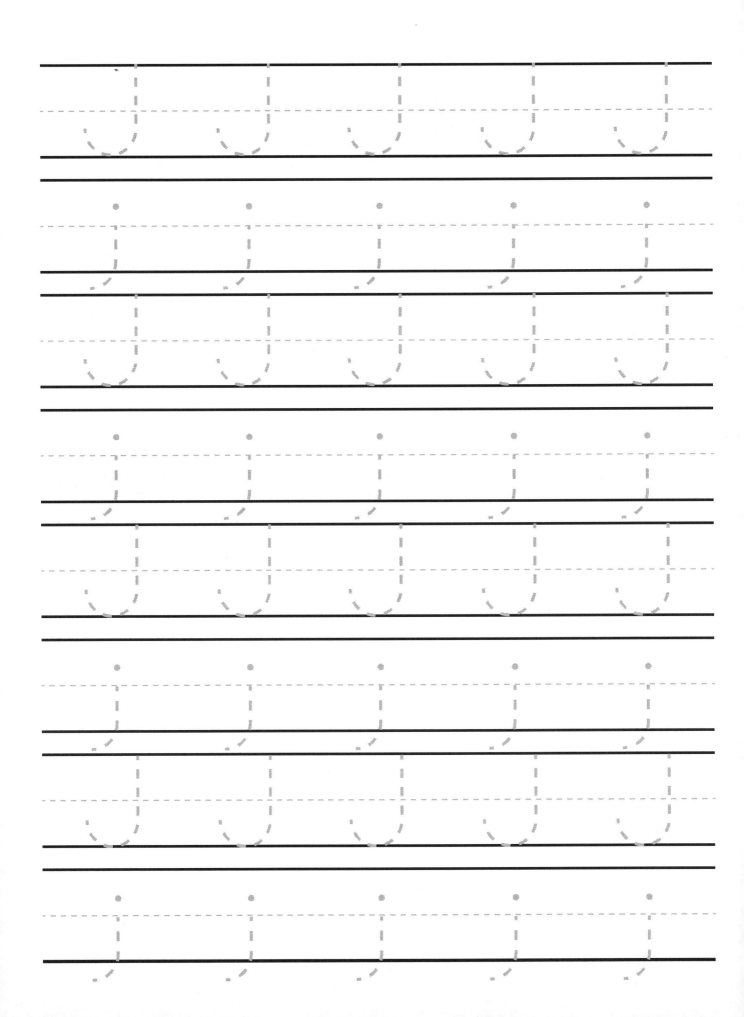

K is for

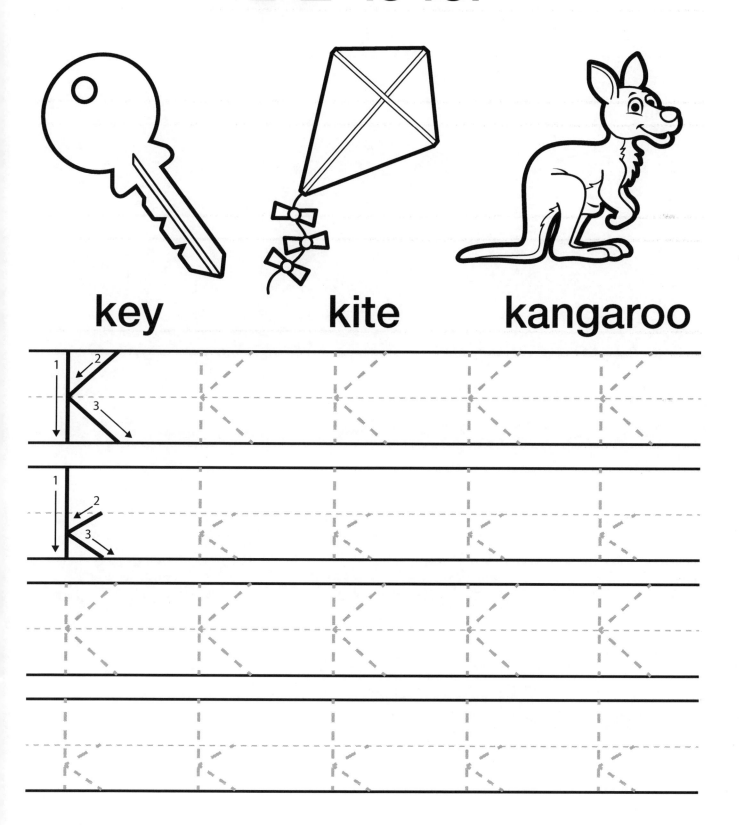

key   kite   kangaroo

L is for

leaf   lamp   lion

M is for

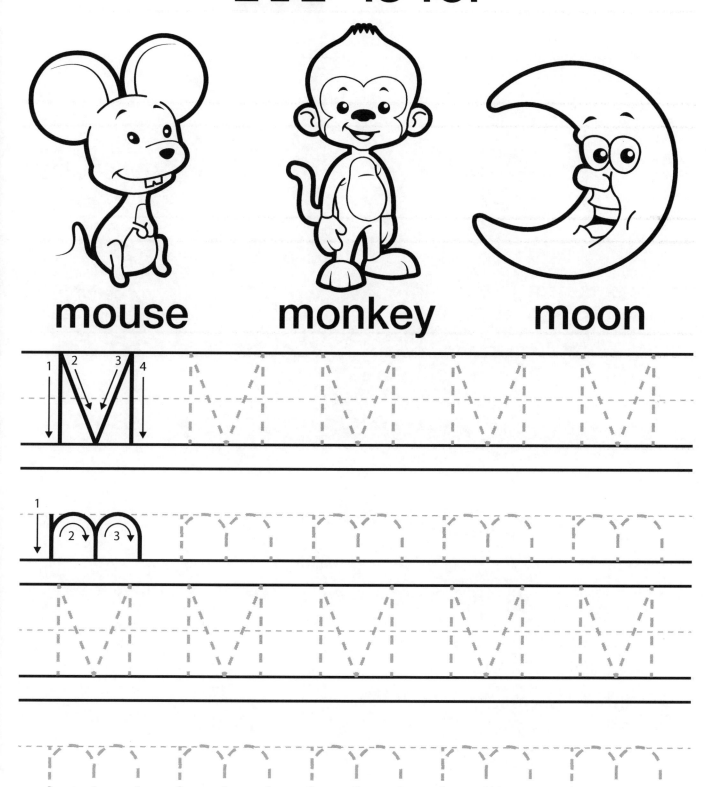

mouse   monkey   moon

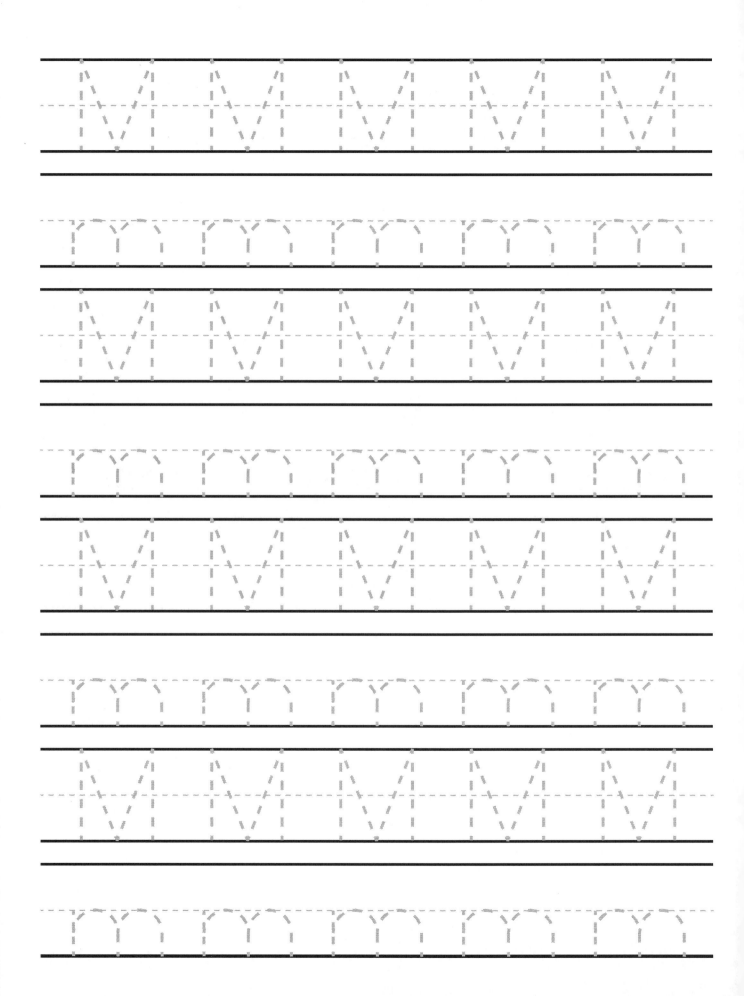

N is for

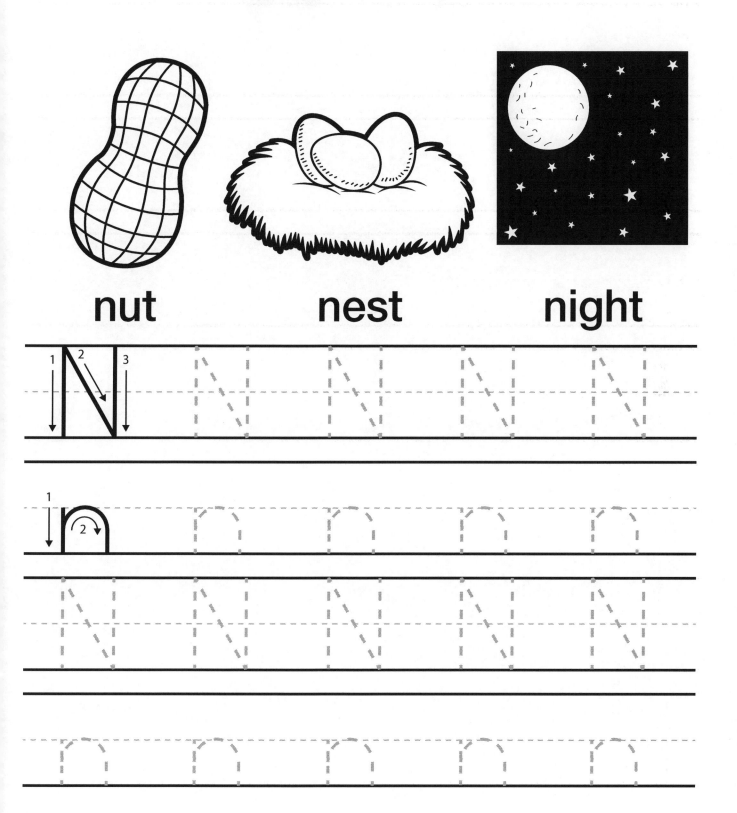

nut   nest   night

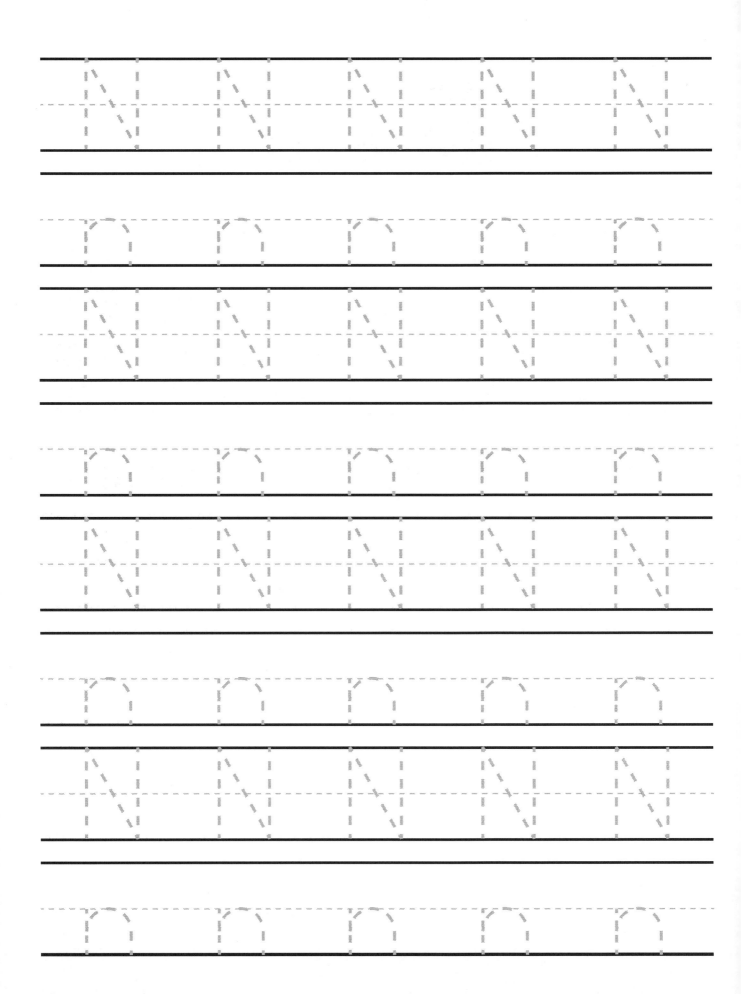

O is for

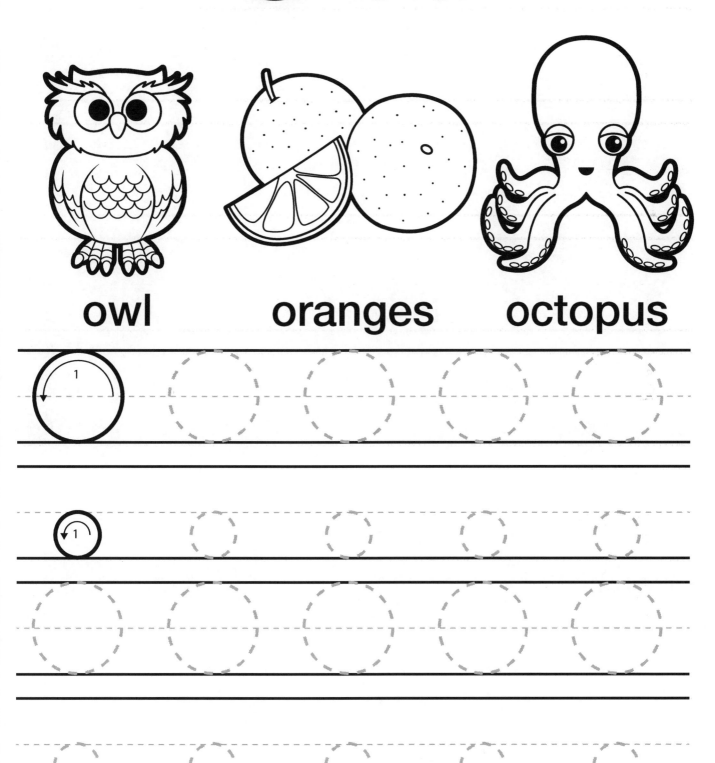

owl   oranges   octopus

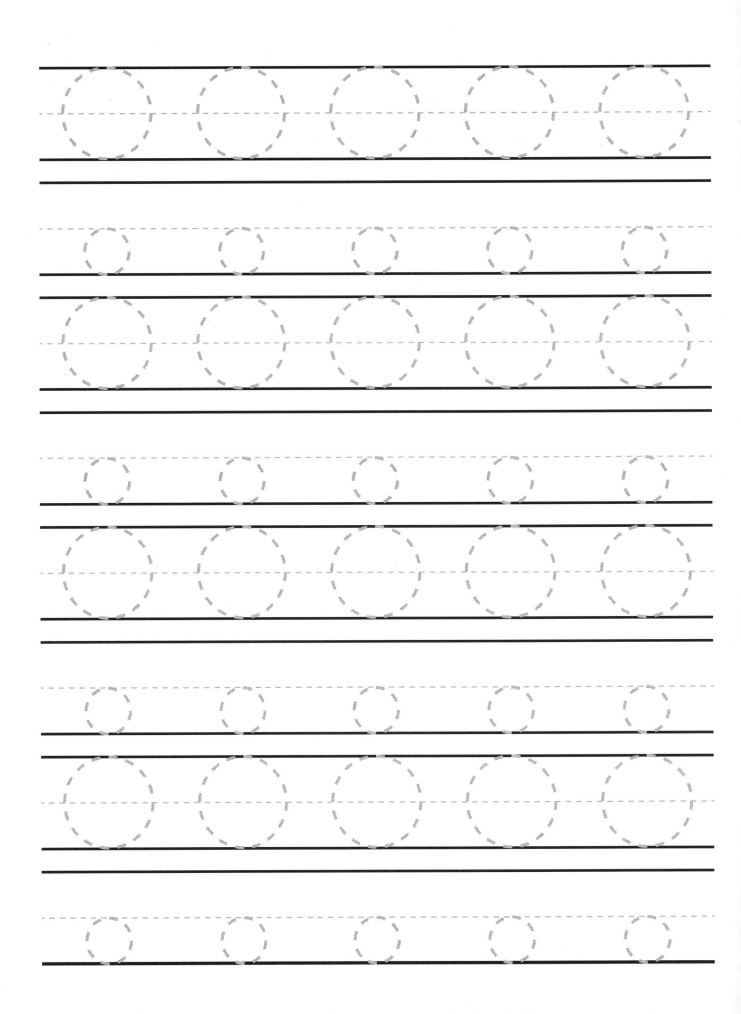

P is for

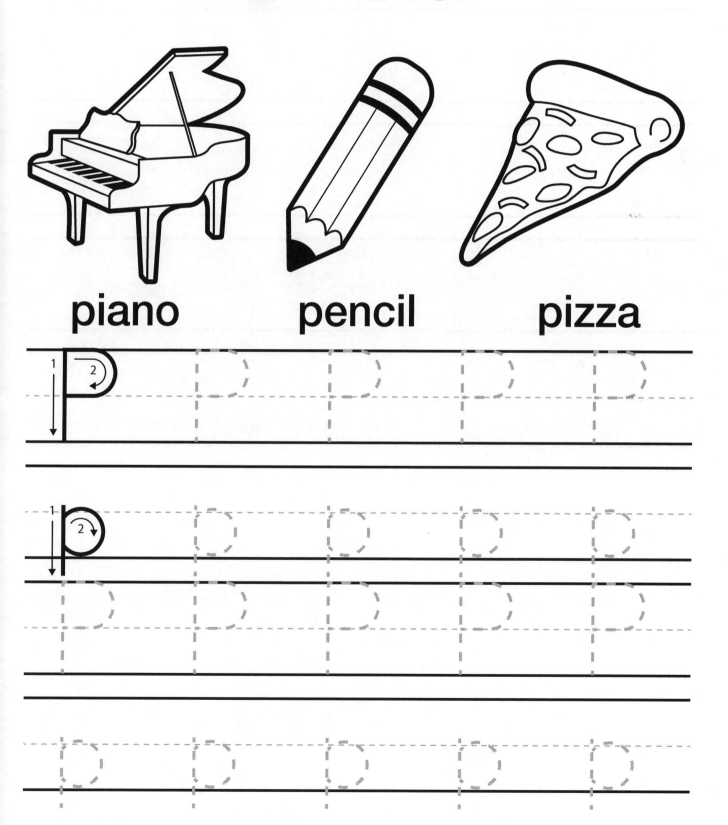

piano   pencil   pizza

P P P P P

p p p p p

P P P P P

p p p p p

P P P P P

p p p p p

P P P P P

p p p p p

Q is for

queen

quack

quiver

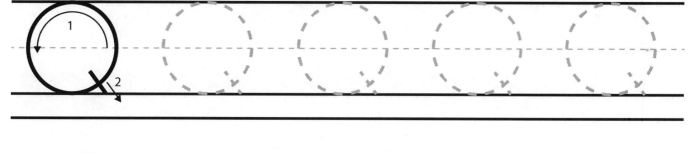

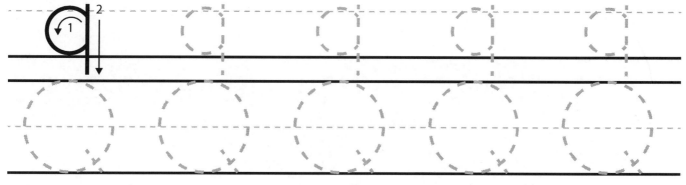

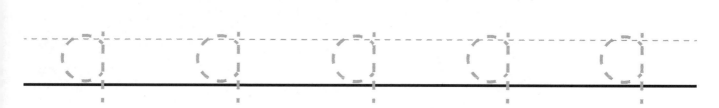

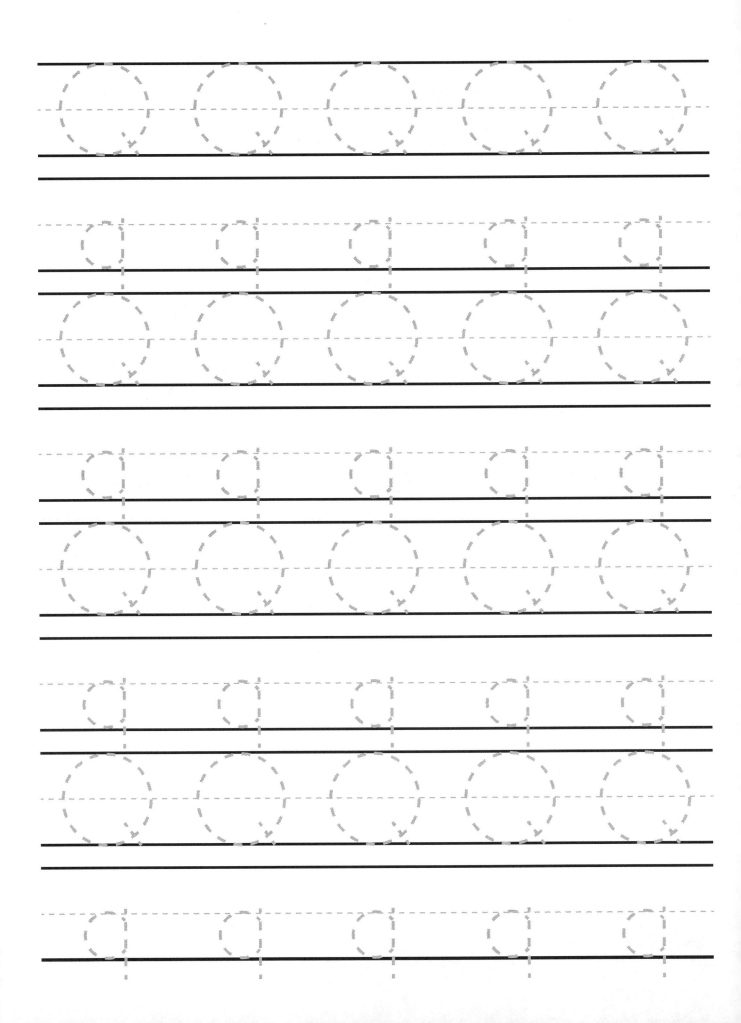

R is for

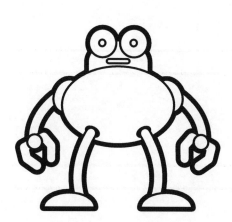

robot   rabbit   rocket

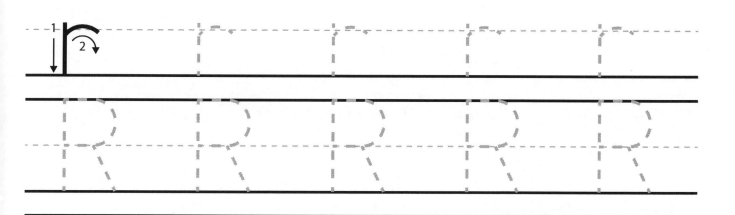

R R R R R

r r r r r

R R R R R

r r r r r

R R R R R

r r r r r

R R R R R

r r r r r

S is for

sun   strawberry   snake

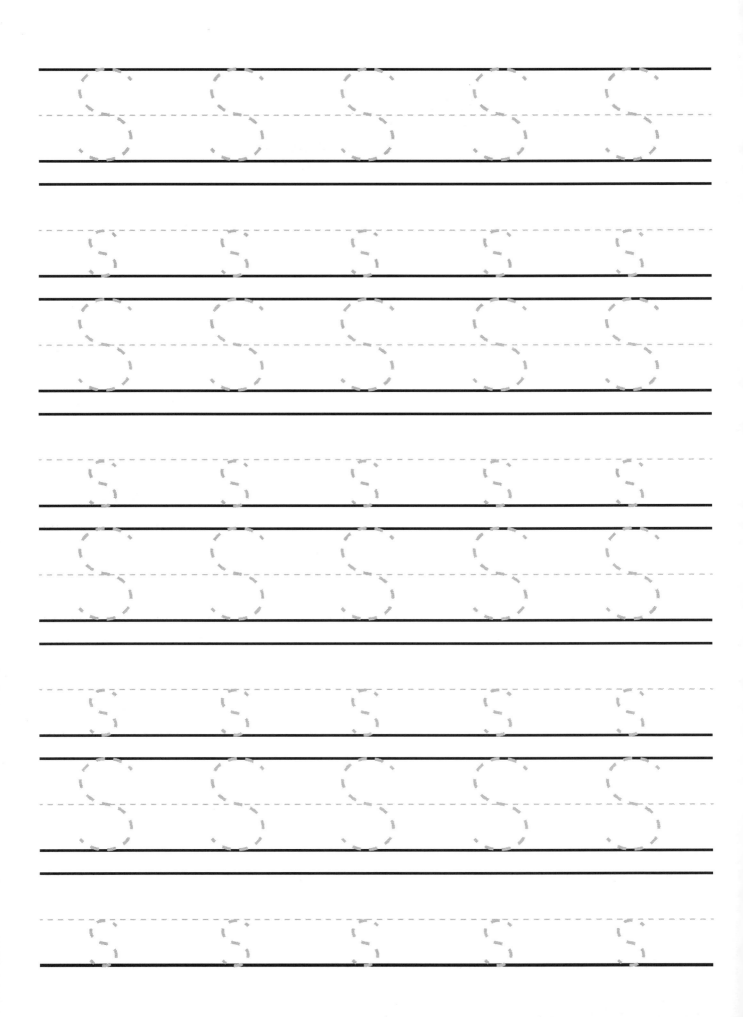

T is for

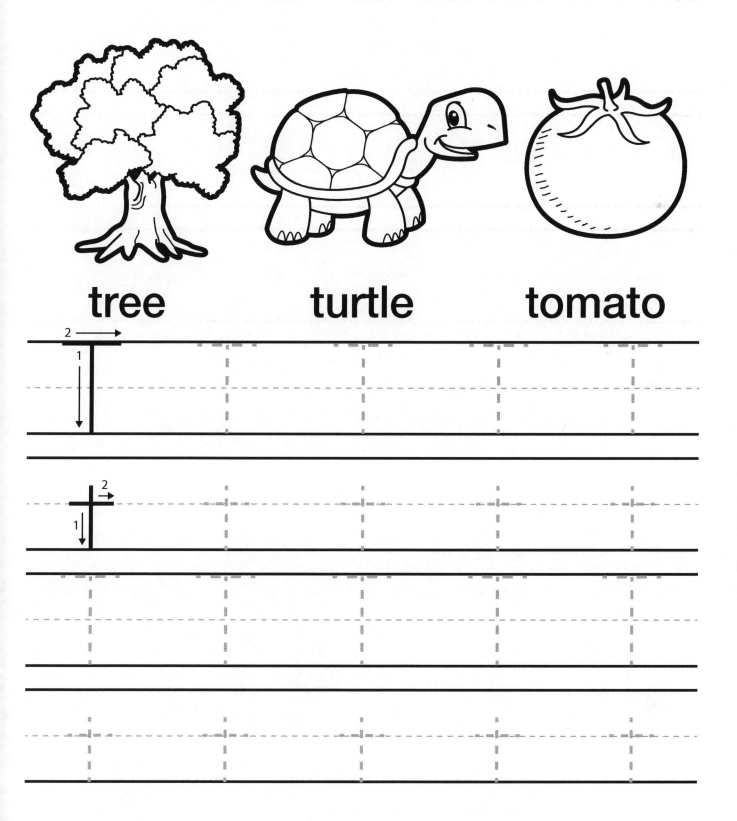

tree   turtle   tomato

U is for

unicorn   umbrella   under pants

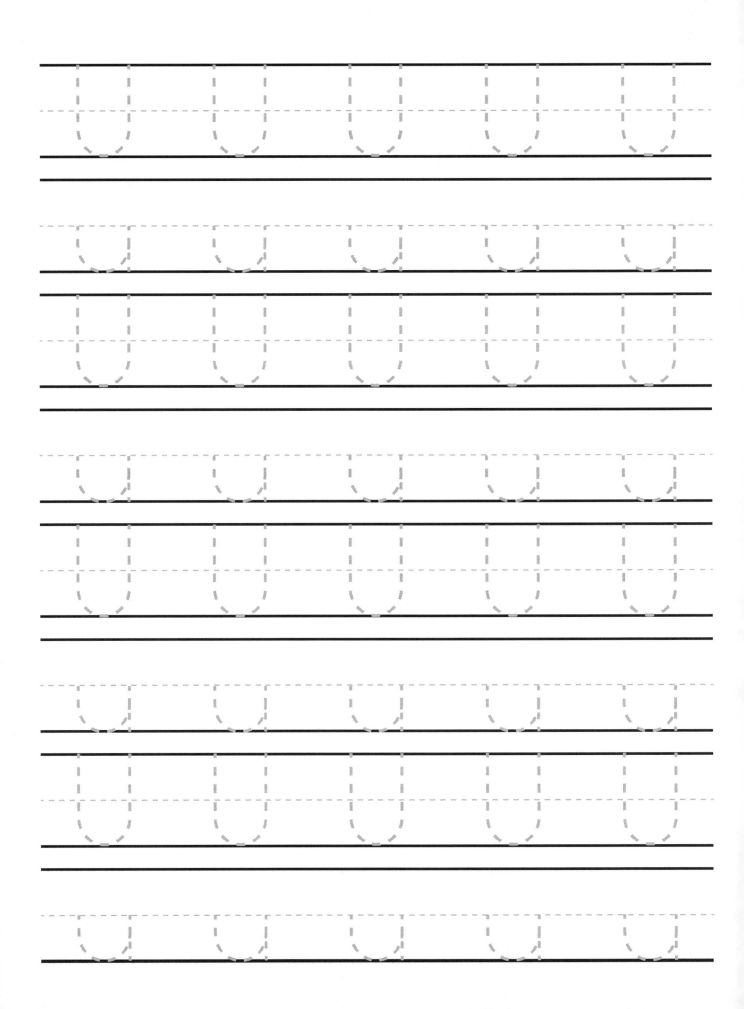

V is for

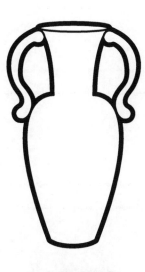

vase

violin

volcano

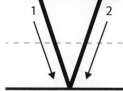

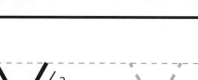

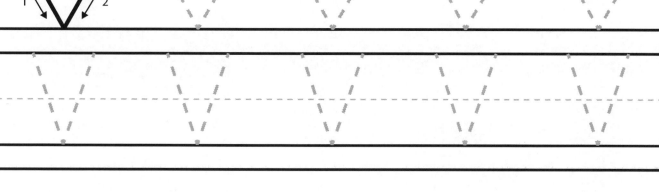

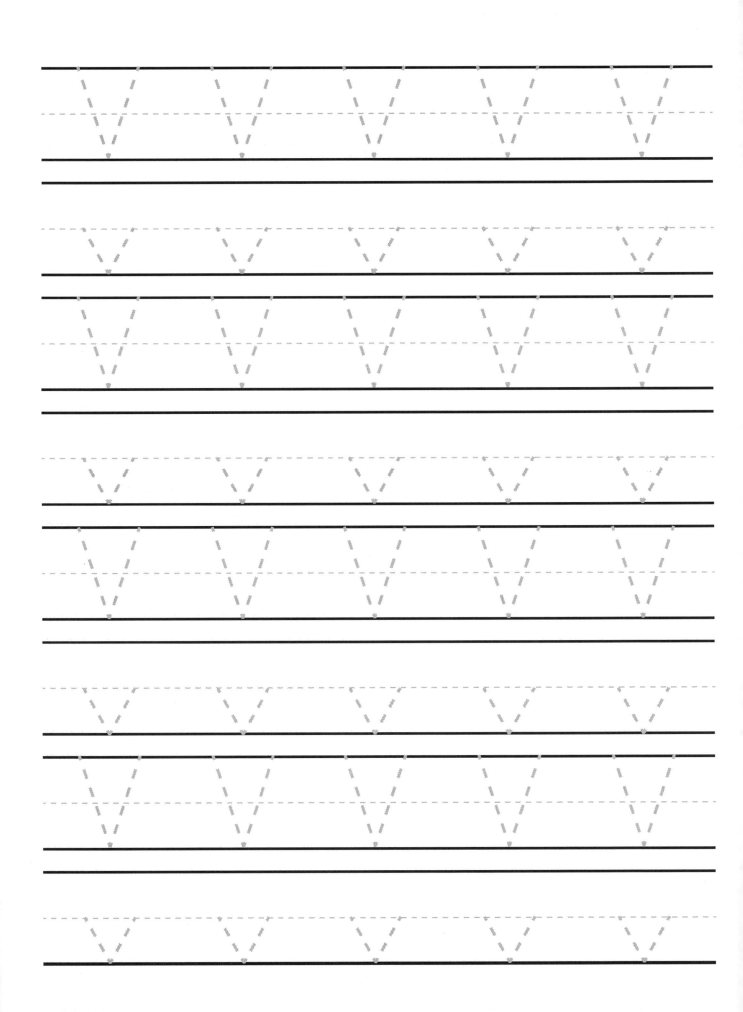

W is for

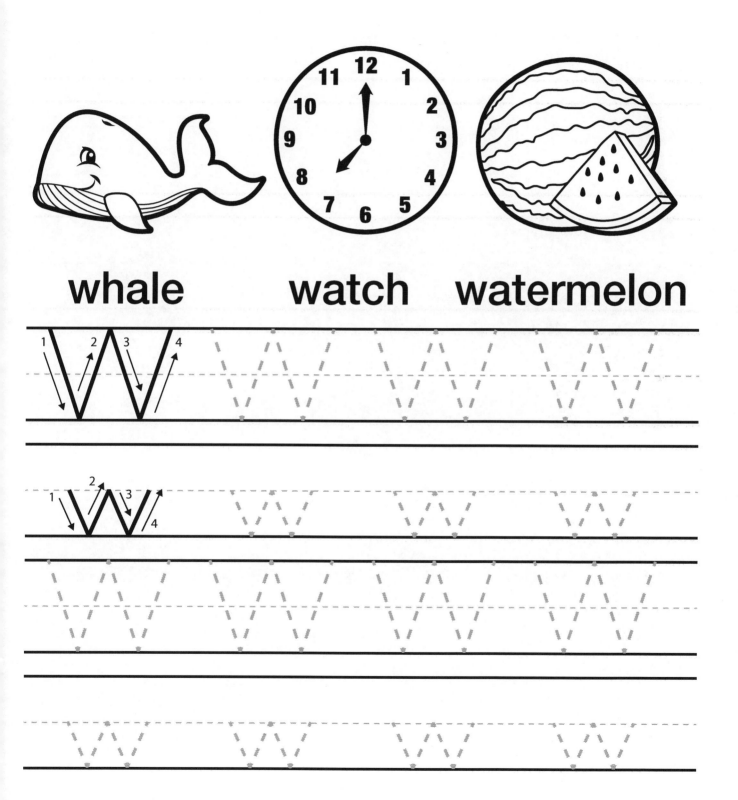

whale   watch   watermelon

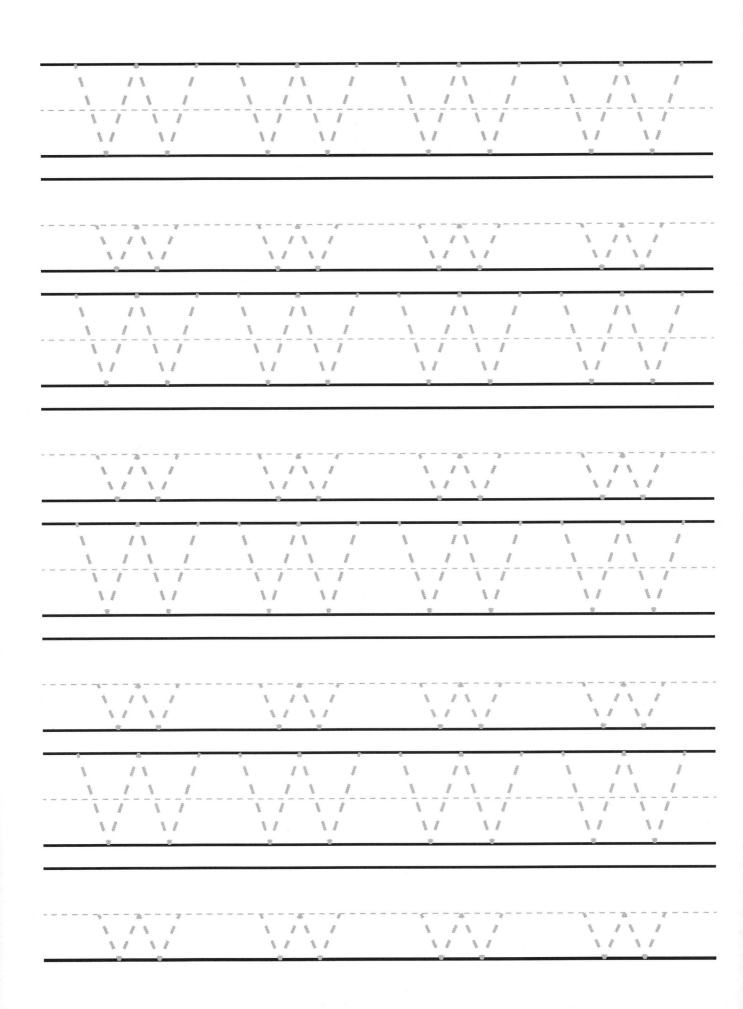

X  is for

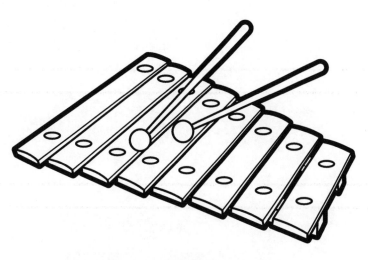

xylophone

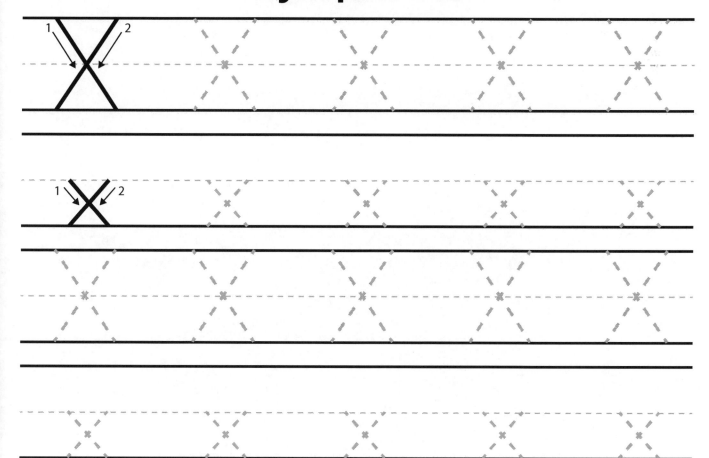

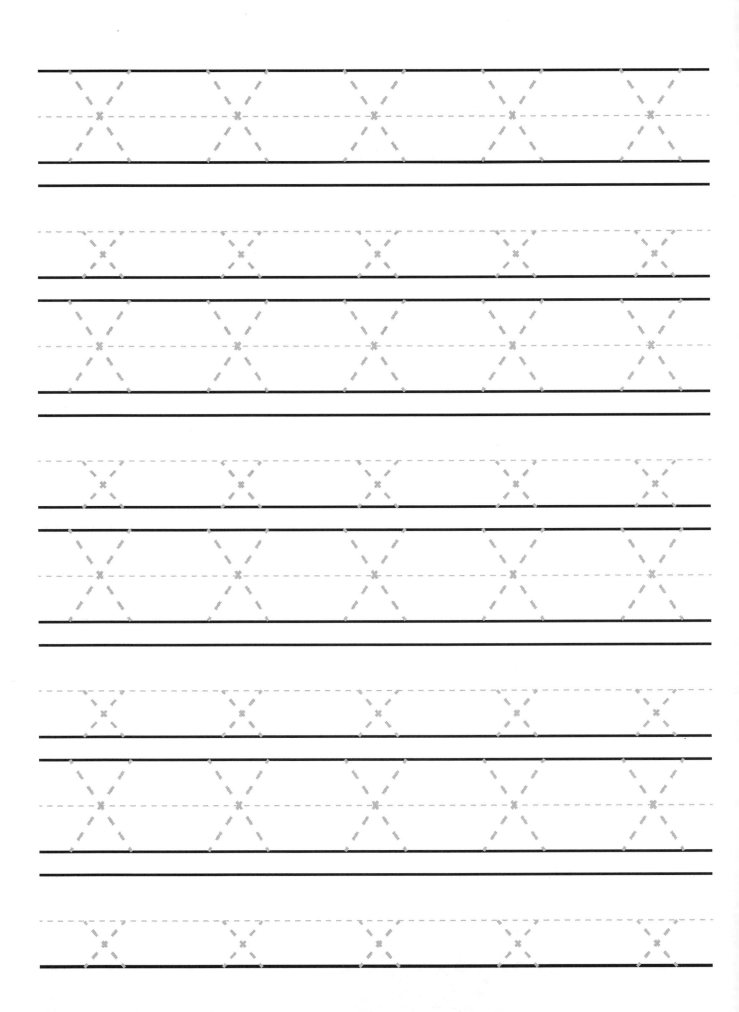

Y is for

yo-yo   yarn   yak

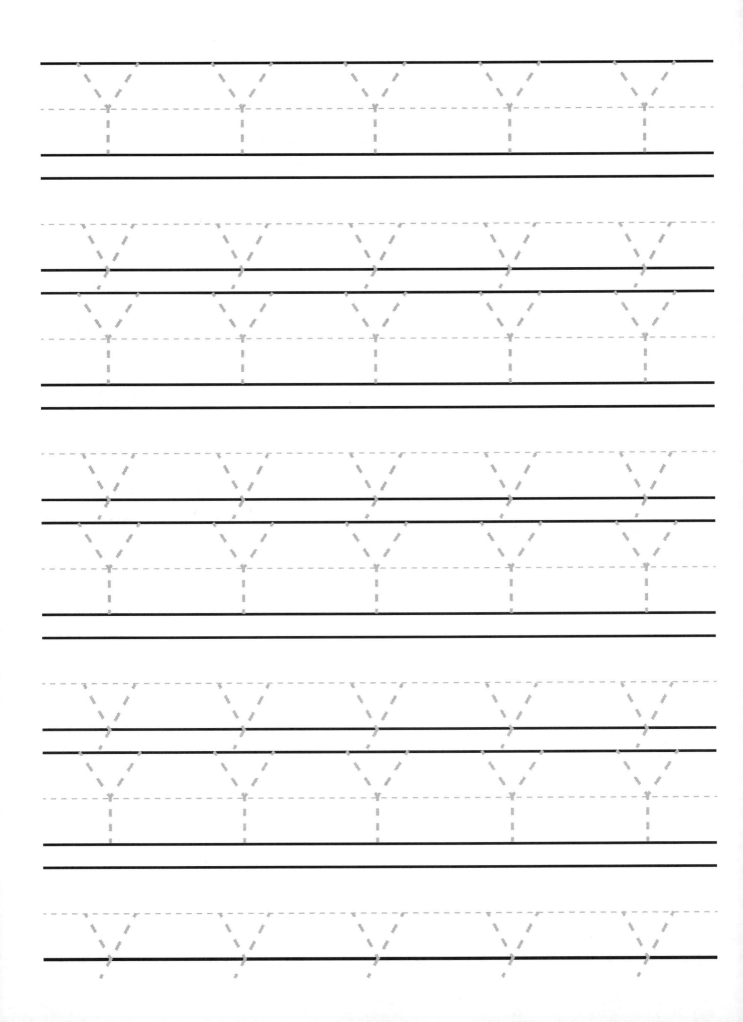

Z is for

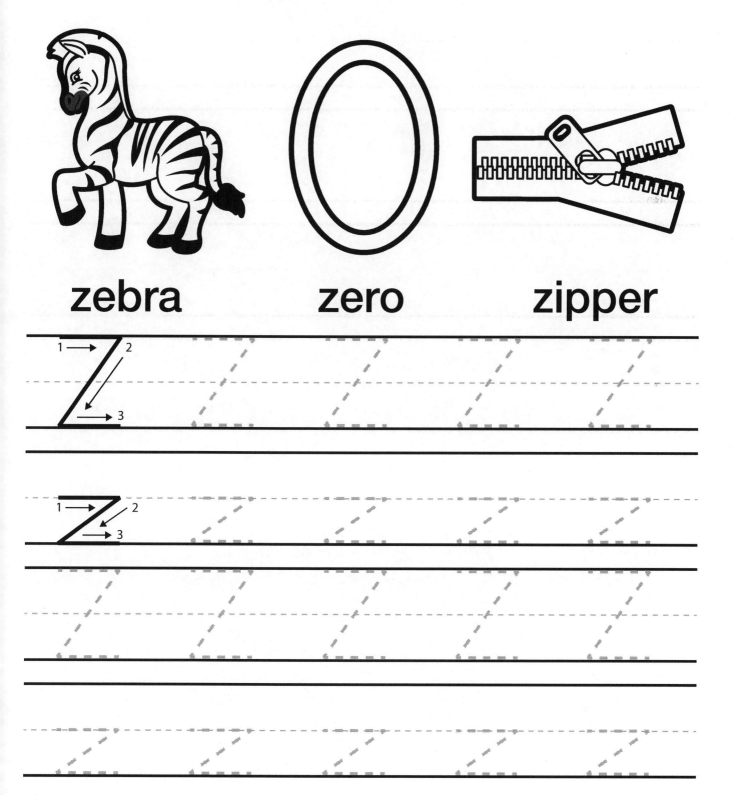

zebra   zero   zipper

3 letter words

cat cat cat

cat cat cat

bat bat bat

bat bat bat

hat hat hat

hat hat hat

mat mat mat mat

mat mat mat

pat pat pat

pat pat pat

rat rat rat

rat rat rat

sat sat sat

sat sat sat

3 letter words

dog

fog

hog

log

big

dig

pig

3 letter words

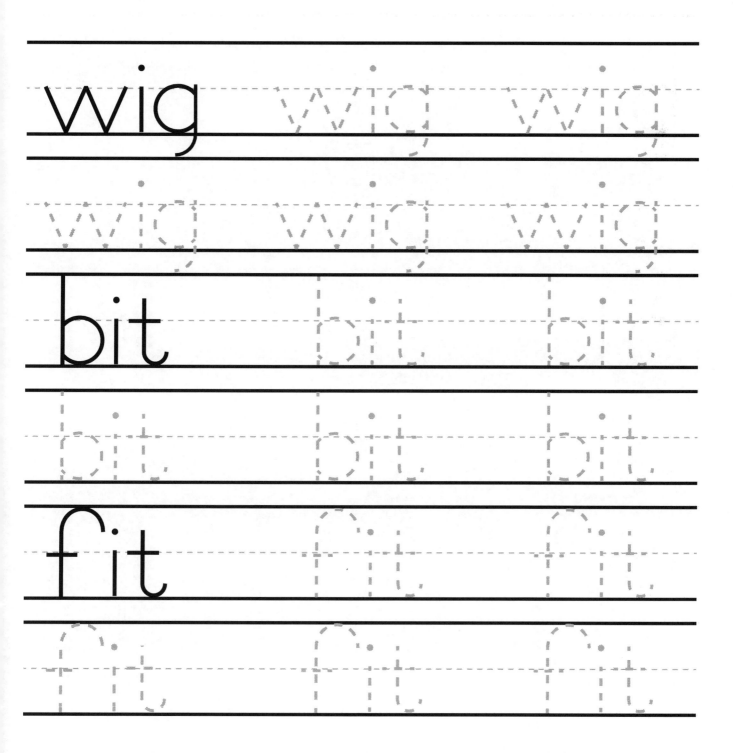

hit   hit   hit

hit   hit   hit

pit   pit   pit

pit   pit   pit

sit   sit   sit

sit   sit   sit

cot   cot   cot

cot   cot   cot

3 letter words

dot   dot   dot   dot   dot

hot   hot   hot   hot   hot

jot   jot   jot   jot   jot

lot   lot   lot

lot   lot   lot

not   not   not

not   not   not

pot   pot   pot

pot   pot   pot

rot   rot   rot

rot   rot   rot

3 letter words

bag   bag   bag

bag   bag   bag

rag   rag   rag

rag   rag   rag

sag   sag   sag

sag   sag   sag

tag _tag_ _tag_

tag _tag_ _tag_

wag _wag_ _wag_

wag _wag_ _wag_

cut _cut_ _cut_

cut _cut_ _cut_

hut _hut_ _hut_

hut _hut_ _hut_

3 letter words

nut   nut   nut

nut   nut   nut

bug   bug   bug

bug   bug   bug

dug   dug   dug

dug   dug   dug

hug hug hug hug hug

hug hug hug hug

mug mug mug mug

mug mug mug mug

rug rug rug

rug rug rug

tug tug tug

tug tug tug

3 letter words

cab   cab   cab
cab   cab   cab

bus   bus   bus
bus   bus   bus

dip   dip   dip
dip   dip   dip

fan   fan   fan

fan   fan   fan

gas   gas   gas

gas   gas   gas

hay   hay   hay

hay   hay   hay

joy   joy   joy

joy   joy   joy

3 letter words

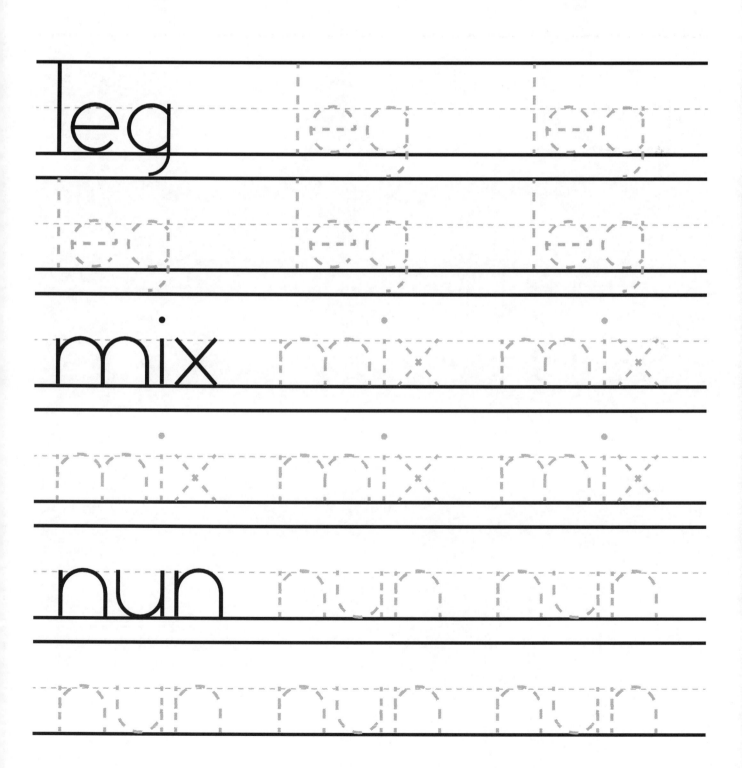

leg

mix

nun

pen   pen   pen

pen   pen   pen

rat   rat   rat

rat   rat   rat

sea   sea   sea

sea   sea   sea

tea   tea   tea

tea   tea   tea

4 letter words

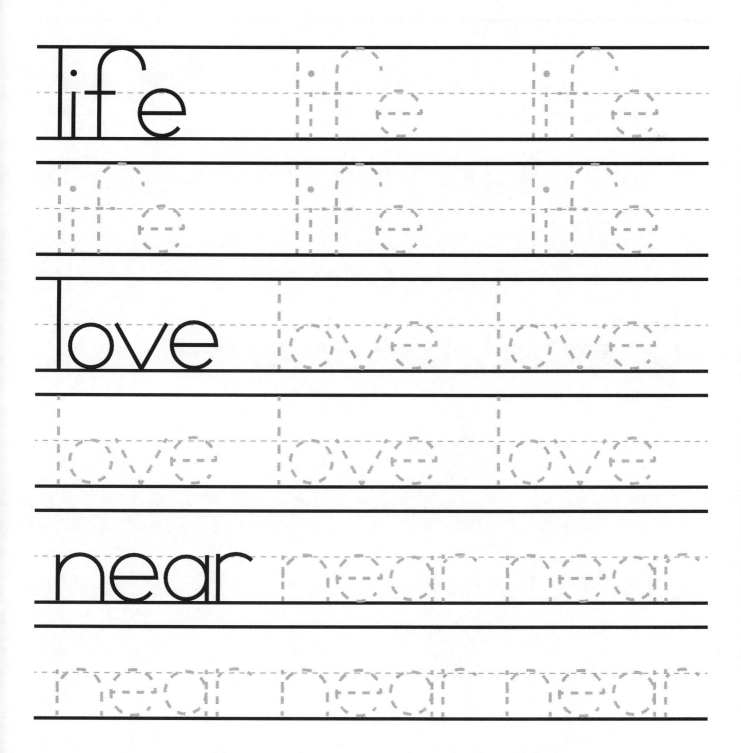

life

love

near

five five five five

five five five

else else else

else else else

tree tree tree

tree tree tree

over over over

over over over

4 letter words

able able able
able able able

have   have
have   have

soul soul soul
soul soul soul

foot

lion

live

safe

4 letter words

pain pain pain

pain pain pain

rain rain rain

rain rain rain

iron iron iron

iron iron iron

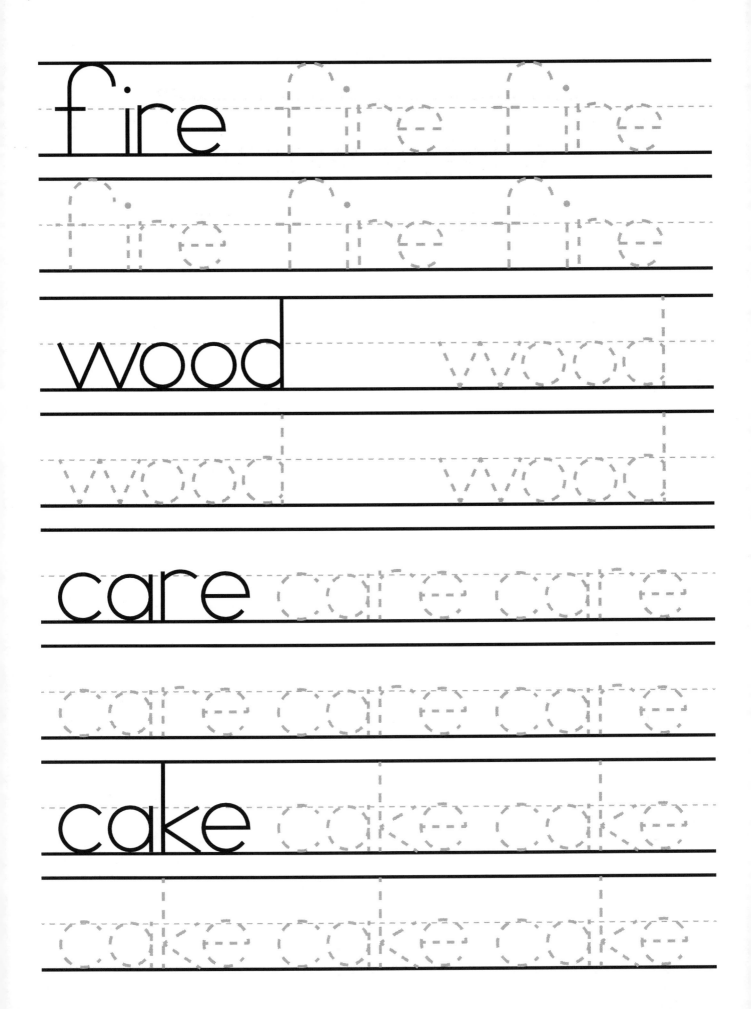

fire

wood

care

cake

4 letter words

away   away

away   away

moon   moon

moon   moon

mole   mole

mole   mole

nine nine nine nine

nine nine nine nine

ring ring ring ring

ring ring ring ring

king king king king

king king king king

fish fish fish fish

fish fish fish fish

4 letter words

sing   sing   sing

sing   sing   sing

star   star   star

star   star   star

city   city   city

city   city   city

rich   rich rich rich rich

rich rich rich rich

duck   duck duck duck

duck duck duck duck

ball   ball   ball

ball   ball   ball

back   back

back   back

4 letter words

lady   lady   lady

lady   lady   lady

self   self   self

self   self   self

work   work

work   work

golf

ally

body

down

4 letter words

land land land
land land land

blue blue blue
blue blue blue

gone gone
gone gone

kite   kite   kite

kite   kite   kite

come   come   come

come   come   come

high   high   high

high   high   high

hard   hard   hard

hard   hard   hard

4 letter words

rock rock rock rock

rock rock rock rock

teen teen teen

teen teen teen teen

rose rose rose

rose rose rose rose

wish

wish wish

wish wish wish

baby

baby baby

home

home home

line

line line

5 letter words

seven

seven

heart

heart

pizza

pizza

water water water

board board

angel angel

green green

5 letter words

music music

music music

three three

three three

mouth mouth

mouth mouth

sugar

dream

apple

laugh

5 letter words

tiger

faith

earth

river river

river river

money money

money money

smile smile

smile smile

lemon lemon

lemon lemon

5 letter words

south south

south south

after after

after after

stone stone

stone stone

about

about   about

again

again   again

piano

piano   piano

peace   peace

peace   peace

5 letter words

house house house

house house

alone alone

alone alone

power power

power power

today

today today

anger

anger anger

phone

phone phone

pasta

pasta pasta

5 letter words

magic   magic

magic   magic

honor   honor

honor   honor

zebra   zebra

zebra   zebra

train

train train

brain

brain brain

mango mango

mango mango mango

under under

under under

5 letter words

eight

eight

thing

thing

light

light

story

story

night

night

glory

glory

candy

candy

5 letter words

puppy
puppy   puppy

plant
plant   plant

smart
smart   smart

jelly

black

dirty

dance

6 letter words

always

always *always*

around

around *around*

better

better *better*

father father father

father father father

garden garden

garden garden

giving giving

giving giving

ground ground

ground ground

6 letter words

letter

little

puzzle

zigzag

zigzag

pizzas

pizzas

jockey

jockey

jackal

jackal

6 letter words

pyjama pyjama

pyjama pyjama

jumped jumped

jumped jumped

object object

object object

junkie

juggle

jugged

bronzy

6 letter words

zipper

zipper

blazed

blazed

quirks

quirks

quiver

gazebo

jogged

gazing

6 letter words

jigsaw

jigsaw

hijabs

hijabs

hazily

hazily

backup

inkjet

jagged

hazing

6 letter words

quakes

jungle

zagged

squeak

juiced

jagged

zigged

6 letter words

fields

fields

pickup

pickup

lizard

lizard

judged

breezy

jungle

equips

6 letter words

circus

injury

chicks

inject

saliva

boozed

expect

south   south

One last thing - we would love to hear your feedback about this book!

If you found this coloring book enjoyable and useful, we would be very grateful if you posted a short review on Amazon! Your support does make a difference and we read every review personally.

If you would like to leave a review, just head on over to this book's Amazon page and click "Write a customer review".

Thank you for your support!

Made in the USA
San Bernardino, CA
10 January 2019